Love Like Love

Kingshuk Sen

Clever Fox PUBLISHING
Chennai • Bangalore

CLEVER FOX PUBLISHING
Chennai, India

Published by CLEVER FOX PUBLISHING 2021

ISBN: 9789391537005

BOOK DESCRIPTION

In this modern-day, our view of love has become so skewed that we are failing to differentiate between pretence and the real deal.

We have built stereotypes about how love should be and how it shouldn't be. To an extent, we have gone to commoditise "love" itself.

"Love like Love" is an attempt to break a few of those notions and myths about love.

More than anything, it's a silent attempt in helping people understand, the most underrated feeling of our generation called "Love".

PREFACE

I bow my head in front of the Supreme Godhead, Lord Krishna.

I have been writing for quite a while now but it's poetry that I have always found the most eloquent way of laying your heart open. It's so subtle but can still be so powerful in touching those broken chords within us.

Similarly, I hope that this subtle pursuit of mine, to help heal all those broken hearts, who either lost love or still longs for it in their life, bears fruit.

Through this work of mine, I have tried to relay the one important message that I realised in love myself. That "love is like fluid as it catches the shape of the heart that holds it and not definitive as we may want it to be. It is above all human sentimentality and frivolousness. It was meant to remain pure and free of any expectations and sense of gratification.

So let us all fall, in the truest form of love. Let us all promise to let "Love be like Love"

In a world full of branded items,
It's Love that comes at a premium.

We all want to be loved unconditionally.
But fail to persevere in Love relentlessly.

In a relationship,
You don't have to be an amazing lover.
Just be a nice person.
That will do the job.

In between those innocent fights.
Stealing glances & Endless chats.
I fell in love with you.

Love can calm down, even the strongest of the tempest.
Within your heart.

If someone couldn't leave you better, than when they found you.
Shame on them!!!

From the pack of all hearts.
It's you that I want,
My queen!!!

Self-love.
Self-care.
Own peace of mind.
When in love, prioritise in this order!!!

When you fall in love, with eyes closed.
That's called a blind!!!
And remember,
That a blind hand always costs double!!!

Just treat all your broken relations,
Like a bad bus ride!!!
Sometimes the experience is bumpy!!!
But ever heard anyone,
Quitting taking bus rides?

When your favourite dream, turns into your worst nightmare.
Then know that the person of your choice,
Was not a fairy.
But you had befriended the devil.

We hold on to grudges than holding onto each other.
We create walls between us than creating memories.
We feed our Ego than letting it Go!!!
&
Then expect Love to thrive!!!
How Naive!!!

We doubt our Soul's ability to connect.
But are confident of finding Love, over a paid network.
Which we are sure, will drop!!!

Treat love with love.
And you will have peace.

Be hopeful of finding "Love",
But never be hopeful about the "outcome of love"
Because love will find its way to you, without you trying!!!
But the outcome, you can never leave something like that to hope.
It will depend, on how hard you want to work for it.

There is no right or wrong way to effectuate "love".
Either you are sincere in your pursuit of love.
Or
You are insincere.
As simple as that!!!

Once the connection between two souls is mutual,
All texts, tweets, and calls
Will cease to exist!!!

If you can't be someone's fondest of memories.
Don't be their worst nightmare either.

You want entertainment in life.
Turn on the 8:00 pm soap opera on the television.
Someone's heart is not something you should play with.

Relationships are like treasure hunts.
There are hurdles.
There are struggles.
There are deceptions.
It's all about your perception.

I asked love,
Why do people grow apart?
Love answered,
Because sometimes, even the most virtuous one,
Can't withstand a disloyal heart.

The trick is,
To not expect anything from Love.
But just to love well!!!

If someone left you, for another person.
They prioritised!!!
So what are you waiting for???

I'll prefer a cup of tea with you,
Over a fine dine.
I'll prefer a walk with you,
Over a car ride.
And will choose you always and for a lifetime.

On those late nights, when the entire city is sleeping.
I would want to hold your hands and stare at the skyline
through the window.
We won't say a word.
Just sit there leaning against each other.
Amidst the silence of the night.

Even the most broken of hearts.
Even the most lost souls,
Yearn for love.

Hopelessness is the real disease.
And Love is the cure!!!

I wake up startled every night, having dreamed of you.
With a hurting head I get back to bed and somehow pass the night through.
Most mornings are lovely, cause it's your messages that I wake upto.
Texts from you, sometimes angry, sometimes caring,
I feel happy that at least you do.

Sometimes, let a few things remain unsaid.
Because even silence is a way to say,
That "I love you"

Regret can be strong.
Ever checked the obituaries? heaped with dried flowers.
All standing testament of lost love.
Just trying to tell us "take care of your love,
while you still have time"

In this age of online romance,
We are missing those hugs and kisses.
Those glances and smiles.
But promises are being made, of holding hands and
walking on for miles.

Just the way, it's the nature of the waves,
To break against the shore.
It's a hearts trait,
To keep falling in love.

Commit to love, not leave.
Commit to being loyal, not treacherous.
Commit to being truthful, not deceitful.
That's the secret recipe of a love life,
Which is blissful.

When in Love.
Let your lover breathe.
Let your lover fly.
Let them spread their wings.
Let them touch the sky.

Love prospers.
When you feed your heart with possibilities.
Love withers.
When you feed your heart with insecurities!!!

If you want your love to give good mileage.
Then ensure to maintain and service it well.
Or else, don't cry about those frequent breakdowns.

In modern day love,,
We are more bothered about the scratches and dents on our cars.
Than the ones, we have inflicted upon each other's hearts.

We expect to find pleasure in Love.
And that's outrageous!!!
Because Love was meant to deliver peace.

We so religiously ensure to…
Change our perfumes,
Change our watches,
Change our wardrobe,
But fail to change our outlook, towards love.

Water your love and it will grow.
Give direction to your love and it will flow.
Real romance takes time.
So have faith in each other and take it slow!!!

What you believe to be as love,
May not be the same love, that others understand.
So hey genius!!!
Don't try to shove your version of love, down someone else's throat!!!

Don't let love haunt you!!!
But heal you!!!

21st-century romance is funny.
We choose our ice cream flavours out of genuine love.
And base our choice of partner,
Out of current unavailability of better prospects.

If someone loves you genuinely,
Don't break their heart.
Because then, you are just not robbing them of their share of love.
But you are robbing them of their ability to trust love.
Ever again!!!

Love is like Dewdrops.
If not appreciated at the right moment,
Will disappear with the rising sun.

Everyone manages to fall in love.
But only a few, manage to hold onto love!!!

In a relation,
Sincerity is a necessity.
&
Sensuality is a luxury.
Start choosing wisely!!!

Always choose the right person in love.
There is no guarantee,
That even the right ones may stay.
But at least, they won't leave you damaged.

Why would you want to break someone's heart?
When you can keep it, nourish it and cherish it!!!

Strive to give someone, the love they never had.
Not the bad memories, which they never had.

Moments of distance feels like ages between me and you.
A minute of silence seems like eternal void separating me from you.
I try to keep my heart tied but each time it breaks loose, at the sight of you.
Then I know it's your love, that I have fallen in and its true.

Do more of these when in love.
Take a walk holding hand in hand.
Rest your head on their lap and take a nap.
Give a peck and whisper in their ear "you are my world".
And promise,"it will always beat for them, and never be sold".

One heart.
One love.
One life.
Sometimes you don't get second chances,
So strive!!!

Never regret having fallen in love, with the wrong person.
Because nevertheless the pain they inflicted upon you,
They did light up your eyes, even if for a moment.

Love is like that one twinkling star, on a stormy night sky.
Trying to fight all the clouds and the wind,
But still manages to twinkle.
Just for you!!!

The day you find the person.
In the presence of whom, you can get naked.
Without taking your clothes off!!!
I guess that's the day,
You can quietly whisper to yourself.
"Love is in the air"!!!

Lost love wasn't bad love.
It was just someone else's love.

It could be at "dawn"
It could be at "noon"
It could be at "dusk"
But love will come knocking at your door.
Just make sure to take a peek.

You think that you are protecting your heart,
By stopping yourself from falling in love?
Then you are wrong.
All you are doing is, stopping magic from happening.

Stop beating yourself up, for that broken relationship.
Which was never meant for you in the first place.
Trust me!!!

Just to heal your own heart,
Never break another one!!!
That's a crime!!!

Matches are made in heaven,
Promises ain't!!!
Those are made here on earth,
And hardly ever kept!!!

Love is like a tempest.
And our heart, a boat caught up in one.
Although the boat knows, that its fate lies away at the shore.
But its sails keep directing it towards the waves.

Good morning!!!
I love you!!
So lift yourself.
Feel the sun on your skin.
Let the breeze kiss your hair.
And above all,
Love yourself a bit as well.

These days it's lust that's been in fashion,
Disguised in the name of love.
And when the lust starts to fade.
We blame the "poor love" to be not true.
But "love" wasn't even there all this while.

Have we ever thought?
That the truest and deepest of love is that of a candle.
It burns itself up, just to light up the darkness.

What if "Love" was never meant to stay?
But just stay Free!!!

Don't let your "last" love,
Be your "last" love.
Because love is just,
More than a person.
More than a heartbreak.
Love is timeless!!!

You don't fall out of "love"
That happens only in the English language.
We fall out of people.
The love, that remains.

We teach ourselves to love.
But fail to learn, how to forgive.
It's like ending up cooking a curry.
But just having forgotten to add, the right amount of salt.

The biggest gifts that we can give in love are truth,
trust, and time.
All the rest, are just meant for decoration.

Sometimes we have to go through a thousand
heartbreaks.
Before we can finally find love.
Most of us don't even last our 3rd.
Just don't give up!!!

One day, when love finally arrives in your life.
You won't be anxious.
You won't be scared.
You will be at peace.
And you will know!!!

Love was always about "trust"
And never about "lust"
Not sure, how we all got it wrong.

We judge love so often.
But don't!!!
Just let it spread upon you, like the morning sun.
Drench you with it's heavy downpour.
And calm you down, with its snowy touch.
Just pure and unadulterated.

You have someone, who loves you unconditionally.
Love them back.
Cherish their presence.
And more than anything,
Just don't let them go!!!

In this world of texts, tweets, and SMS.
I want to be that handwritten " love letter" to you.

You stole someone else's love.
And you expected it to last with you???
Really!!! Think again.

You are something more than lovely.
You are something more than sweet.
You are something more than beautiful.
You are really my own heartbeat.

Love for me is,
Returning home after a hard day's work.
And melting in your arms.
Lying down in your lap,
While you caress my forehead with your fingers.
We talk and I can't remember when I fall into a deep sleep.

Real love will cost you nothing.
No gifts.
No coffee dates.
No dinners.
Absolutely nothing!!!

When you chose me because of my car.
Don't expect me to hold onto you,
Just because of your soul.

In today's world of Instagram & Facebook,
We say "I love you" a lot.
But just that, we mean and feel it a lot less.

Yeah, it's fine not to love someone back,
Just the way they do.
But don't break someone's heart, into a million pieces.
That they have to spend an entire lifetime,
Just gathering it back.

Choosing love based on "looks",
Is a perfect recipe for disaster.
Ever seen a liquor bottle???
Looks a 100th time more glamorous than a medicine jar.
But ever heard?
One saving a life?

Every heartbreak,
No matter how big or small, needs closure.
But if you didn't have one?
That means you are still going to sleep every day.
With the demons of your past.
And trust me!!! These demons won't let you last!!!

Define love?
Two people making honest efforts and endless compromises.
To ensure that they continue to stay together.
And yeah, one more thing…
They don't lie!!!

You can be completely ignorant of love,
And still, be in it.
That's the beauty.

For me,
My sense of loyalty.
My sense of trust.
My peace of mind.
Is more important than you!!!
So don't make me choose!!!

If in a relationship, you were made to choose.
Over and over again!!!
Prove yourself over and over again!!!
Then sorry dear,
You mistook a "job" for "love".
And that job wasn't even paying you!!!

Wake up every day.
Just to fall in love, with the same person.
Over and over again!!!

You can bury those demons of your heart,
Only using the bricks of love.

The biggest thing in love is intent.
If you intended to create timeless love.
You will receive romance, over and above.
But if you intended to gratify your desires.
All you will ever receive in return is deceit.
And nothing more.

Bad love is like a car without an engine.
It doesn't do you any good.
Just sits there and costs you, your peace of mind.

Choosing to continue with a bad relation,
Is like smoking a cigarette.
We all know, it will eventually kill.
But that immediate kick of nicotine is too addictive to part with.

These days love is about,
People showing off their partners, like objects.
And I wondered,
When did exposing our most private parts publicly,
Become fashion?

Your blinking eyes put even the twinkling stars to shame.
I have fallen in love with you,
And it's my heart to blame.

Heart is that window,
Love is that cloudy sky.
All you ought to do is,
Hold one another's hands and fly!!!

Break the stereotype around love,
Not love itself.

We make room for the right kind of plants,
Within our homes.
But fail to create spaces for the right kind of people,
Inside our hearts.

Never default on an EMI of the heart.
Because you may get back a foreclosed house,
But not foreclosed love!!!

The irony of human creation is.
High rises are fitted with elevators, to lift us.
While we fail to lift,
Someone's heart, soul, and spirit.

We spend months, choosing the right kind of decors for our bedrooms.
But are so flaky while deciding,
Whom to let inside it.

A bad lover is like alcohol.
All they add up is empty calories.
But zero nutritional value.

Difference between love and lust?
Lust restricts you!!!
&
Love liberates you!!!

I saw an angel passing by.
With her shades on, open hair, under the blue sky.
Pink dress, bow on her hair and wearing flats.
She kept walking and I said "oh look at that"
Jaded eyes carried the calm of the sea.
I knew that I had fallen,
In love with thee.

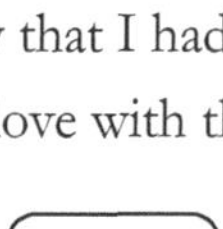

If you gave your heart to someone,
Depending on their riches.
Then it's like, getting sold to your highest bidder.
And that's called auction, not love.

Even the strongest of love goes through wear and tear.
But when most choose to give up on each other.
The real companions are busy,
Stitching up each other!!!

Choose wisely, as what you want your love to be?
Endless and Timeless?
Or
Hopeless and Loveless!!!

When you let love be your compass,
You can never be lost!!!

Even a cup of tea, when sipped in haste.
Can burn your lips.
It's the same with love as well.
Give it some room, to breathe.
Some space to flow
A little time.
&
It will grow!!!

We all want to leave our footsteps in this world, isn't it?
Then let's leave the ones,
Which can be retraced back to love!!!

It's not the fonts that matter.
But the content, that defines a book.
Similarly, it's not glamour that matters.
But the beauty of the soul, which overrides all looks.

The right notes can create a symphony.
The wrong ones create noise.
Similarly in love as well.
The right notes can create romance.
While the wrong ones wreak havoc!!!

We, humans, are so driven by this underlying "devalued" sense of self.
That we reject the people who accept us, considering them as unworthy.
While we chase the people, who keep rejecting us.
Considering them the real deal.

Love sometimes seems so beautiful,
filled with the brightest of colours.
While sometimes it seems so ugly and dark,
showing the truth like a mirror.
Sometimes it's the sunshine,
Showering warmth all around.
And sometimes it's the falling star,
shattering hearts to the ground.

Love is like a crispy buttered toast.
All it requires is,
A generous sprinkle of sugar!!!

Love is that space,
Where two souls are content.
In each other's embrace.

Love is a valley with its ups and downs.
But it's also got,
Rain, sunshine, and rainbow.

Side effects of modern-day achievements?
Protein is getting bottled as "powder".
Fake cheese is getting branded as "cheddar".
While love is getting "cheaper and cheaper".

I asked my heart,
Why are you scared of falling in Love???
The heart replied,
It's not about the heartbreak,
But the nightmares that will follow.

We are so deluded by the looks.
That we forget to look into their heart.
The signs of breakage were always there.
It's just that,
We chose to ignore it from the start.

Our notion of love itself is so misplaced.
We proudly advertise the long list of lovers,
Whom we dated.
But foolishly overlook that one real relation,
Which was fated.

Don't try to hide those scars that you got in love,
with the band-aid of hope.
Walkout of a toxic relation immediately,
Before you keep sliding down,
That slippery slope!!!

There is nothing wrong,
In having unconditional love for someone.
But just ensure that,
You don't start to lose your existence,
In someone's presence.

Don't let someone's snowy touch,
Grow your heart cold.
But love them back with so much warmth,
That you become a story,
Worth to be told!!!

Choose to be the superhero of your own heart.
There is nothing more helpless,
Than holding your bleeding heart, waiting to be saved.

Our problem.
We want love to be that cheap and fast "ready to eat" meal.
But want it to be,
Healthy, tasty, and feisty at the same time.

Proudly wear those scars of your relationship,
Like a million-dollar attire.
And just laugh it off every day,
Like a cheap little satire!!!

Let your love be like a donut.
Chocolatey on the surface.
Crispy underneath.
And soft from inside.

Get high in someone's love,
Not their lust!!!

The only thing that separates humans from animals,
Is the sense of love and compassion.
But we seem to have miserably failed at that as well!!!

If someone finds that one reason to love you,
Go find another hundred,
To love them back!!!
That's real reciprocation.

Always choose the right DJ for that party called "love".
Because the right ones,
Will make you feel alive with their buoyant tracks.
While the wrong ones,
Will kill your vibe with their lament.

If you will be my kite,
I'll be your string.
You promise to hold my heart,
And I promise to be your wing.

We choose to create our memories,
Either they can be hurtful and painful.
or
Can be cheerful and blissful.
So next time someone hurts you in love,
Forget them like that pleasant dream.
Yes, it will pain that the dream got over.
But your lips will still twitch into a smile,
At the thought of them.

Never settle to remain, a chapter in someone's book.
When you can be your,
Own endless poesy.

The evilest of hearts has the power,
To kill the most vibrant of souls.
So think twice before,
You let anyone within your fold!!!

Those devilish ones, who come into your life,
Disguised as a lover.
You can say it from the start,
That there is a sense of negativity around them.
To an extent that,
they themselves can't be happy in their own company.
Always look for those signs.

In a chessboard full of pieces,
Choose to be the pawn.
Who will travel across the board, and transform
themselves into a queen.
Just to be with their King!!!

Beware of those trojans!!!
Who comes to you offering love.
And once you lend them the access.
They will hack your heart.
Corrupt your soul.
And hold you ransom for the love they installed inside you!!!

Love is like a wholesome meal.
It should leave you fuller and make you feel whole.
Not leave you in bits and make you feel in pieces!!!

These days fitness and diet are in fashion,
While genuine love has gone out of date.

It's my heart, not your garage.
That each time you drop by, you get yourself repaired.
But leave me emptier than the last time.

In love.
It's hope, which is the only constant.
Rest everything is fleeting!!!

Don't burn the entire love story, of your imagination,
Just because of a heartbreak.
Rather keep the story,
Just change the characters.

You don’t need to be sure about, everything in life.
The only thing that you need to be really sure about is,
Whom are you falling for in life!!!

The moment two people fall in love,
They no longer are just mere human beings to each other.
But rather, they become custodians of each others,
Heart, Soul, and Spirit.
And they need to protect it.

In love,
Sometimes people spent decades together but still
remain, strangers.
And sometimes even a moment of interaction,
Feels like an eternal familiarity.

If you ever have to choose between loving and
respecting,
Choose respect.
Because choosing to respect is a conscious choice.
While love, is incidental to respect!!!

Like the falling snow, never enough for the mountains.
The blowing wind, not enough for the trees.
And the way breathing never enough for us to be.
A lifetime of love is not enough, between you and me.

In this age, when relationships are breaking like
chocolate chip cookies.
We need to glorify those couples,
Who are fighting it out daily, to be together.
Who wakes up every day, to just be in love with the
same person.
And for whom just another day with their lover,
Feels like a lifetime!!!

Cheating in love, Is like eating fritters.
It tastes really good.
But is damn unhealthy for your heart!!!

Always keep a track of your bank account, called heart.
And don't let anyone withdraw,
more than they ever invested in it.

Start choosing your partner based on,
How well they treat you.
And not how good they are in bed with you!!!

Love is a luxury,
Which not all can afford!!!

You don't have to offer flowers to impress someone.
Just offer the right vibe!!!

Prioritise love because you consider it to be a priority.
And not because of your insecurities.

Stop treating love,
Like a game of rummy.
And you won't get dealt,
A lousy hand!!!

Top five wrong reasons to fall in love these days.
I'm getting old, who will take care of me?
All my other friends have a partner, so why not me?
I need someone to flaunt and go out with me.
I just had a breakup so need a distraction for me.
Let's play with someone's heart until I find a better match for thee.
And then you have those few narcissist assholes,
who just love to see people getting hurt.

Love is like a choir.
You don't need to sing perfectly,
But just sync perfectly.

It's you and only you, all around I see.
In the blowing wind, falling rain and in a bit of me.
Even the clouds and the birds can't escape the magic you do.
I smear my hands with ink, just writing about you.

Being in love with the wrong person,
Is like trying to call the right person.
Through a dead telephone.

Stop analysing love and start living it more.
Not always you need to know,
What's there in store.

The day you catch the right wind in love,
Love will blow you away like a fairytale.

Love is like that heavy downpour.
White sheets of water all across the horizon.
Tiny droplets of water creating vapour on the glass window.
A view so breathtaking and serene.

Keep your heart open and give all that you have.
May be love is in giving and never to have.

Hold onto your lover,
To make their life better.
Not bitter!!!

To all those heartbreakers around the globe.
Don't feel too proud of that long list of people,
Whose hearts you have played with.
Because all you are doing is, creating a world full of heart broken people.
Who will never trust love again the same way,
To choose from!!!

I wish you the stars,
I wish you the sky.
Fairies be your allies,
You spread your wings and fly!!!

Love is like that tree in a season.
It changes it's colour,
Sheds it's leaves.
But still rooted with hope,
For the spring to bloom.

Have we ever thought?
Maybe the love that we don't have today and so long for.
Is the result of we having so subconsciously given it up.
In exchange for something else!!!!!

It's fate of a heart to fall in love,
Fate of a river to meander.
So once you find that one true person,
It's not an opportunity, meant to squander.

What are we?
The remains of a fragile past,
Or
the sign of strength saying that we stood tall.
We are what we think,
Because everyone for once, takes a fall.

Loving someone is like showing gratitude.
For trusting you,
For believing you,
And for being with you,
When the rest of the world gave up on you.

Proposal in love has become more like a sales pitch these days.
Nothing legit to offer for the heart.
Everything is running only on packaging!!!

You deserve to find love, unconditional, loyal and trustworthy.
You deserve to find that person, who will love you just the way you are.
Just reciprocate love, the way the world has never seen.
Just stop hating people for the way they are and the things they have done to you.
Just go out seeking never ending love,
And the rest won't matter.

These days we find time to Surf the internet.
But fail to find time,
To Surf each others hearts!!!

Treat your love like "religion",
And you will never be disheartened.
Keep treating it like a gamble,
And you are sure to "stumble"

Through the long summer of deceit, disloyalty, and distrust.
Always ensure to keep your heart
hydrated with the potion of love.

Like the pouring rain all across the plains and mountains.
Thundering lightening peeping through the clouds' curtains.
And the moving storm turning the earth into a cradle.
It's your dreams, that wakes me up with a startle.

Just stop playing all kind of tricks!!!
And gift someone the most inexpensive present call Love.
To win their heart.

Heart is like that northern star.
Never break one,
And it will never let you wander away far.

Just have faith that love is on it's way.
It may take a year,
It may take a decade.
But it will find it's way!!!
And once it arrives, it is meant to stay.

The real distance in a relationship,
Is not the one that can be measured in miles.
But the immeasurable length of silence,
Which lasts between two souls.

Stop seeking everyone's love.
Stop seeking everyone's validation.
Because not all are worthy of your love,
And granting you accreditation.